Zurich. The fina[...] treasures that are nothin[...] vaults. The city's artistic heritage as the birthplace of Dadaism remains vibrant today in the reformed industrial spaces that host its fresh galleries. Post-industrial restaurants are joining a dining scene that reflects a long history as a cultural crossroad. And nightclubs with no closing time vie alongside classy cocktail bars and raucous havens drawing in half the Swiss population every weekend.

While many stop off in Zurich on their way to the Alps, the city itself has a feast of natural attractions within easy reach, from swimming spots on the lake to mountain hikes offering different vistas depending on the season.

Some local legends have shared their side of the city. A curator of a dynamic gallery, a musician behind Zurich's go-to club, a playwright and performer, a culinary expert and a top product designer... A feature story delves into the dark side of art and finance and a short story penetrates the perfect surface of the city. It's all about original minds and the creative vibe. Get lost in the sights, sounds and flavours of the city. Get lost in Zurich.

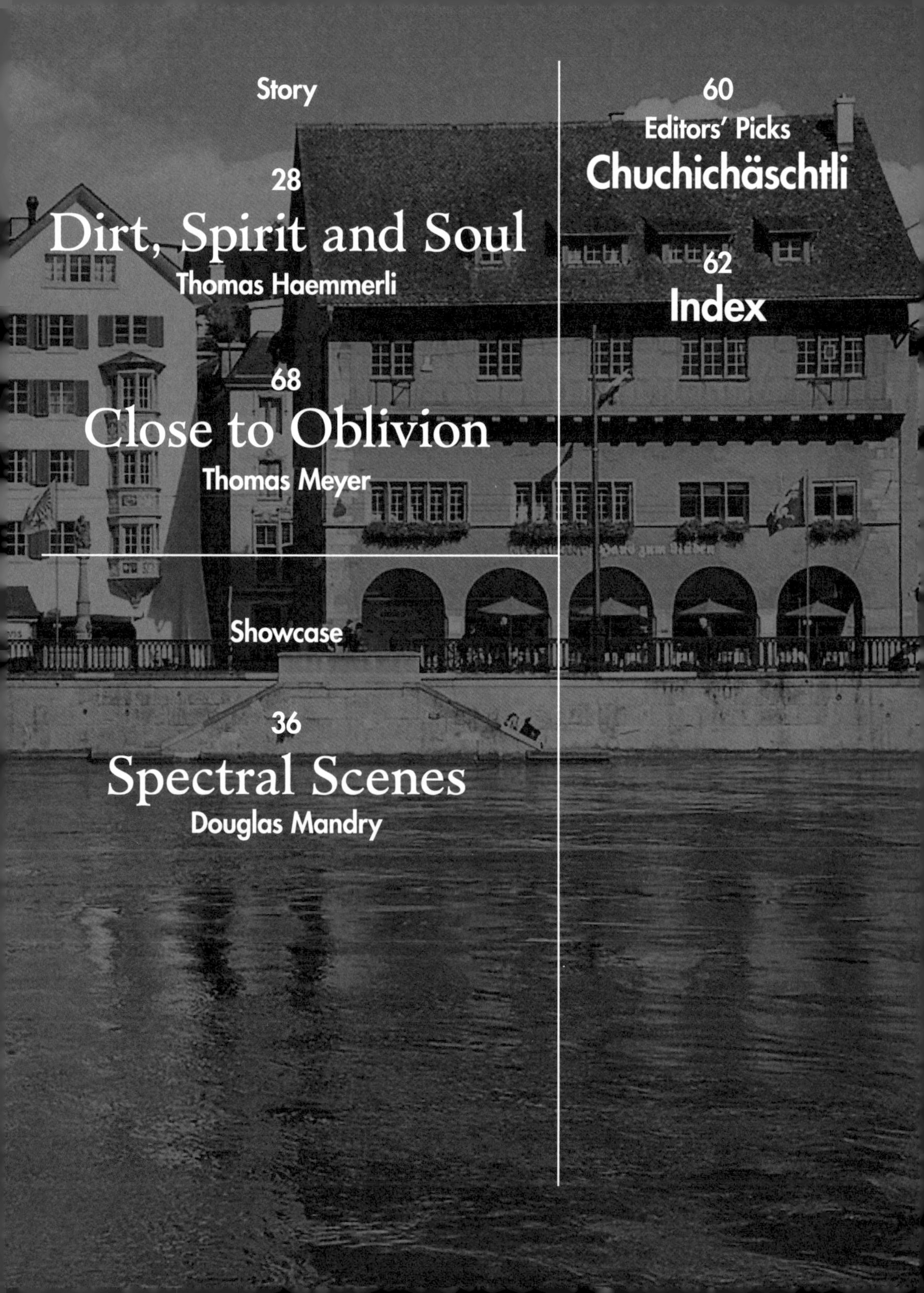

"Those who know animals can protect them", is the motto of *Zürich Zoo*, and the keepers are rather proud of their mini-renderings of natural habitats for the resident 360-plus species. For example, the Kaeng Krachan Elephant Park (pictured) was built to resemble the pachyderms' Thai habitat. Designed by Markus Schietsch Architekten, the giant tortoise-like wooden structure contains sweeping sand, rock and water features for the eight elephants living within.
• Zoo Zürich, Zürichbergstrasse 221, Kreis 7, zoo.ch

It's not just a stopover to ski—Zurich has plenty of stunning nature nearby. And while the seasons sometimes dictate where you can go, a lot of trails are perfect for both winter and summer. From Klusplatz in Kreis 7, depart to *Wirtschaft Degenried*. Then, choose multiple routes through the surrounding woods of the Adlisberg mountain. Atop its 700-metre peak climb the 1954-built wooden observation tower Loorenkopf (pictured) and drink in the gorgeous trifecta of city, lake and Alps.
• Wirtschaft Degenried, Degenriedstrasse 135, Kreis 7, degenried.ch

From Secret Swimming to Post-Industrial Arthouse

Beyond the Banks

Night | Future Perfect

It's not the wall of dice or the mesmerising disco ball collection that make *Club Zukunft* special. It's the spirit. Laid-back but fully committed to its musical standards, the venue is considered by many a dance music-head as the jewel in the city's clubbing crown. The entrance is tucked in a passage by Bar 3000 (pictured), which is the de facto smoking room for Zukunft and also part of the party. But the real action takes place down in the basement, and goes on until morning light.
• Club Zukunft, Dienerstrasse 33, Kreis 4, zukunft.cl

Culture | **Powerhouse**

Harbinger of the Kreis 5 revamp from industrial zone into one of the most richly textured neighbourhoods in Zurich is the monumental *Toni-Areal* building. EM2N architects transformed it from a milk processing plant into a labyrinthine block coursing with cultural currents. The wavy metal façade might trick your eye. And the internal squares and mini "streets" are intended to befuddle the boundary between city and building. Inside, find part of the *Museum für Gestaltung* (Design Museum). The Toni-Areal is hosting its temporary shows, ranging from industrial design to photography, while the museum's main home is refurbished. Meanwhile, the University of Arts (ZHdK) hosts a variety of cultural events including in several mindblowing concert halls. There's a wonderful—and public—university library on the fifth floor, a shop to peruse posters and a canteen for snacks. Just don't miss the view from the rooftop garden over the changing face of Zurich.

• Toni-Areal, Pfingstweidstrasse 94, Kreis 5, zhdk.ch

| **True Originals**

In squeaky clean Zurich, one shopkeeper at least isn't afraid to get a bit of indigo dye on his hands. Roger Hatt first brought Japanese denim Evisu to Zurich 15 years ago, and today his basement at *VMC* is dedicated to blue jeans—with neat piles of everything from 501s to 11MWs. But even the non-collector will find relief in the vintage shirting, outerwear and grand selection of leather boots that fill his heritage store. A few doors down, but still deeply rooted in timelessness—and time, as it turns out— is tiny vintage watch shop *Uhren Atelier*. Seeming almost an old-school kiosk whose main responsibility is to distribute gum among passersby, the atelier is actually filled with hundreds of restored timepieces. Don't be put off by the cheaper models in the window— earn the maestro's trust and he'll unveil his sleek 1970s Omega Speedmasters and classy IWC Pilot's Chronographs.
• VMC, Rindermarkt 8, Kreis 1, vmcoriginal.com; Uhren Atelier, Rindermarkt 21, Kreis 1, uhrenatelier.ch

Food | **No Country for Old Fish**

You'd think second-generation owner and chef Cäsar Meyer would be the one responsible for the daily menu at *Gasthof zur Sonne*. But in fact, it's mostly dictated by local fisherman Samuel Weidmann and Lake Zurich itself. It's not that they don't do meat and game, they do—and it's all sourced from the surrounding regions. But in the end they mainly rely on Weidmann's skill and Zürichsee's caprices... And so should you.
• Gasthof zur Sonne, Seestrasse 37, Stäfa, sonnestaefa.ch

Outdoors **See Life**

Blink and you'll miss the ivy-lined *Männerbad Schanzengraben* (Kreis 10, pictured), a secret, magical place whispered through generations of urban swimmers. The only downside is that it's only for men. But frauen fret not—an enchanting haven of sun-bleached wooden planks and refreshing waters is just for you at the *Frauenbadi* (Kreis 1). Both the segregated lidos turn into popular bars come dusk—with both genders admitted. But for those who want some co-ed dipping, go for the classic vibe at *Seebad Utoquai* (Kreis 8). The 1890-built bathing spot is a classic throwback. For something more natural, head to secluded *Seebad Katzensee* (Kreis 11) just upriver from Zürisee's massive shores. You'll share tanning space with birdwatchers, but the water is warmer.
• Various locations, see Index p.62

Culture **Virtually Virtuous**

As evident in this small-scale museum, you don't need a lot of physical space for a couple of terabytes worth of art. Also clear Is that .gif files can create a more complex dialogue than the usual typed-out banter on the internet. Zurich's *Museum of Digital Art* occupies a single floor dedicated to the digitally programmed art of one solo artist or collective at a time. Though the initial four exhibitions were curated by the museum's board, the subsequent shows are selected and announced exactly how you'd expect from a museum that thrives on the digital: with an algorithm. An interesting process given that it is unaffected by applicants' age, gender, nationality or financial status.
• Museum of Digital Art, Pfingstweidstrasse 101, Kreis 5, muda.co

Marina Olsen
She belongs to the newer wave
of curators who have set Zurich
alight in recent years, having
set up Karma International in
2008 with her partner Karolina
Dankow. "Kar" and "Ma" each
completed a PhD in art history
and their gallery focusses
on international artists working
across various media

Marina Olsen, Curator

Artful Dodger

Marina briefs us on Zurich's artistic panorama, from an extravagantly decorated police station to a new gallery for young, edgy artists. To feed the body as well as the soul, Marina also reveals a chilled-out tapas place with oldtimers, and where to eat steak tartare with your eyes on an original Picasso

How does Zurich's thriving art scene square with its conservative image?

Zurich is an international hub, which makes it connected, not provincial and isolated. One could call it conservative, but we'd describe it as a city with a rooted culture and tradition. Culturally, it's a charged place. Even during the early avant-garde it was home to many protagonists. So it's had a thriving art scene for at least a century!

What does Karma International bring to the collage?

In the 1990s the contemporary scene was defined by curators and institutions still around today—like Eva Presenhuber, Hauser & Wirth, Bice Curiger and others. This generation were responsible for the city's art credentials today. With *Karma International* we wanted to create something new—to make artists of our generation visible. At the beginning we worked on a local scene and bringing artists not shown elsewhere. Now we've opened a space in LA to extend our context and create a new dialogue.

What are your favourite among the other galleries in the city?

There are many and I visit almost all of them. For historic art, the most thrilling is *Galerie Bruno Bischofberger*, just outside the city in Männedorf. This is one of the oldest galleries, which brought Warhol to Zurich. For many years it was in the city centre. But now they have opened this new venue, which is like an institutional space. That's where to see all the big names. The legendary *Thomas Ammann Fine Art* also shows great artists, also from that period, like Warhol and Cy Twombly. It's in a bauhaus villa in Zurichberg—the famous area overlooking the city.

What about for more edgy contemporary art?

One to look out for is a cool non-profit space called *Up State*. It's really experimental and shows young artists who don't have a gallery yet, even ones still at school, or really young artists from abroad. Because it's not an institution, they can be fast, spontaneous and flexible in their choices.

Is there any notable public art?

By the lake you can find "Heureka" by the late Swiss artist Jean Tinguely. This is a huge mechanical sculpture with dynamic machines—definitely a Zurich icon.

And which artists interest you today?

For a year we've worked with the young Zurich-based painter Urban Zellweger—his surrealist, obscure paintings are very intriguing. Currently we're preparing a solo show with Emanuel Rossetti. He's informed by architecture and is designing a stage-like display setting for our gallery. Also look out for Vittorio Brodmann, a young Swiss painter from the newer scene. He works with a cartoonish style that is really unique.

What about an interesting spot for a snowy day?

What's really fun—where I often take visiting artists—is a huge hall in the main police station of Zurich that was painted by Augusto Giacometti—cousin of Alberto. We call it the "Blüemlihalle" ("hall of little flowers"), or the *Giacometti Murals*. To see it you have to show your passport to the police guards, and then you see this amazing painted space. It's really impressive—people love it a lot. Another place to visit is *Kronenhalle*. It's a famous bar and restaurant, but it's also like a small museum, with lamps by Giacometti and paintings

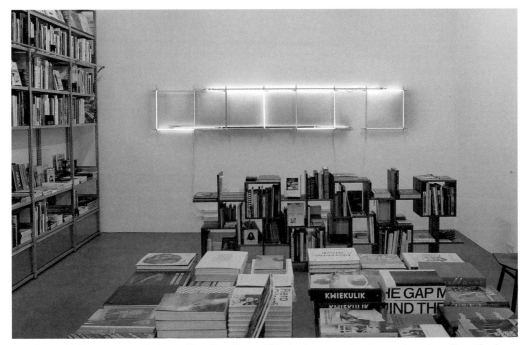

Part of art publishing giant JRP Ringier, Buchhandlung Kunstgriff is ripe for a marathon browse through quality art books

by Braque, Chagall, Picasso... It's designed by the famous Zurich architect Robert Haussmann and it feels like you're sitting in a boat. It's really great to have a drink there. It's a treasure.

Is there any architecture to pass by?
During modernist times Zurich was an important place and one reason was the art historian couple Carola and Sigfried Giedion. They brought Le Corbusier, Brancusi, Aalto and James Joyce here. Next to their private villa they built a certain kind of residential houses with Marcel Breuer—you can still see them around Zürichberg.

Where do you pop out for a good lunch?
My absolute favourite is *Bodega Española* in the Old Town. You sit outside and eat tapas—it's always

really easy. They have a great atmosphere—it's these old Spanish guys who love their job and old Zurich people who go every day. It's not the young, cool thing, it's more to experience everyday life. Just round the corner from our gallery, *Markthalle* is also a wonderful place. They have different stalls—cheese, fish, meat— and a great restaurant with food that's typically Swiss, but a bit more elaborate. For big groups *Volkshaus* is great. It used to be an old shitty restaurant like in every town, but they've redone it in a cool way—they put some neon but kept the old furniture.

What about for other cuisines?
Bimi and *Sala of Tokyo* have the best Japanese. The best Swiss food in the suburbs is *Obere Flühgasse*. My favourite traditional Italian is

Da Michelangelo and a great romantic spot is *Luca²*—a new place with modern Italian cuisine.

Where would you go for a big dinner to celebrate a successful opening?

I have to say Kronenhalle again. I always have the steak tartare there—they bring the ingredients and make it in front of you. But they also have the best schnitzel. It's triple the normal size and the meat is excellent. I wouldn't eat there if you don't eat meat—don't take the fish, take the Chateaubriand or the Robespierre… It's not cheap but it's very elegant. You can also go for lunch at three in the afternoon. It's not on the menu, but order the cucumber salad—it's one of their specialties.

What are the best clubs or bars to get lost in?

Longstreet on Langstraße is the best. It has a really great crowd— it's always about the people who do it. They have the best music taste; they're really up to date. They bring good DJs and they're really connected to the art scene.

Where would you go for clothing?

A new shop, *Tasoni*. They have all the best young brands from abroad that we didn't have before, like Kane, Vaccarello, Puglisi, de Vincenzo. It's not the usual big brands—they've brought the most promising cutting-edge designers to Zurich.

And for vintage?

I'd go to the flea market, *Flohmarkt Bürkliplatz*. It runs every Saturday from May to the end of October. They have great vintage things—the sellers are really mixed. You can buy things like old watches, too. Zurich isn't like New York, we don't have a good vintage scene in shops. Instead people take their stuff to the flea market.

And for books?

Kunstgriff is the only place to go for art books. You can also have coffee or a beer there and it's close to all the museums and galleries.

How would you like Zurich to change in the future?

I'm happy with how it is. I'm a big Zurich fan because it's a small city but really international as so many people travel here, even just for one night, and it's really luxury. There's such a good art scene, with museums, curators and schools, so people are attracted from abroad. That's why it's great to have a gallery here—it's easy to get an audience. Working here feels like you're in a spa, because it's really a healthy place. You have everything you need somehow but it's on a small scale. And then you can quickly be anywhere in Europe— London, Berlin, three hours by train to Paris…

What would surprise first-time visitors?

It depends on the season, but in the summer I often hear that people are fascinated by the opportunity of the lake and the river that everyone swims in, day or night. I don't think that's so usual for a city. Many people go to the lake in the morning for a quick dip or they do yoga—or in the evening you jump in the lake and then go home. That's something like a miracle in the summer. In winter it's mostly grey, but then it's nice that in one hour you can be skiing. There's also a mixture of historical beauty in the Old Town, then the edginess of Kreis 4, with a lot of clubs—so there's many different views of the city.

Good fashion is a form of art... Or at least that's how it's presented in Tasoni's shop window

Under the Uetliberg

The formerly working-class neighbourhood is one of the city's most multicultural areas. Bordered by the city's very own mountain, its diverse streets ooze colour

Food | Fresh and to the Point

In a city sprinkled with Michelin stars, it can be hard to find humbler, yet well-thought-out cuisine. *Vereinigung* (pictured) offers a menu concoted from local and regional ingredients—many organic—and combining traditional Swiss dishes with the slow-food treatment en vogue across Europe. The owner is a merry presence in this soulful place, which is tastefully decorated and features an art nouveau fireplace. Along a similar bent, relative newcomer *Beiz* also abides by a market-fresh philosophy, with a small menu that provides cold cuts and cheeses to bridge the early evening gap. The no-frills décor emulates the dishes, eschewing unnecessary elaboration. The hearty fare is accompanied by a generous wine and beer selection, including tasty local brew BFM. There's even fish fingers on the menu—a kids' comfort food redone with a soupçon of culinary adventure. Stoke a bit of extra gluttony and attack the desserts: copious crème brûlée, a much-talked-about lemon pie or even hot waffles with fruit compote and cream might prevent any need for a midnight snack.

• Vereinigung, Manessestrasse 132, Kreis 3, vereinigung-barsol.ch; Beiz, Zweierstrasse 114, Kreis 3, restaurant-beiz.ch

Ida y Vuelta

The recently redone Ida Platz has become a
focus for the new energy bringing Wiedikon to
life. The places dotted around include *Piazza*
(pictured)—a thoroughly chilled-out spot for brunch,
snacks or an aperitivo. Another little treasure
is *Bei Babette*, that serves up crêpes and gallettes
in savoury and sweet form. This French feel
extends to games of pétanque in the square and
a villagey, continental feel when the weather
is not too gruesome. If you're digging the
outdoors vibe, just buy a beer from the kiosk,
sit on a bench and soak it all in.
• Piazza, Idaplatz 2, Kreis 3, ida-piazza.ch; Bei
Babette, Bertastrasse 16, Kreis 3, beibabette.ch

Food Blooming Neighbourhood

Binz is a mini-neighbourhood within Wiedikon,
and its concentration of creative agencies has
caused a flowering of local eating options.
One such flower is *Daizy*, which is buzzing with
pro- fessionals for coffee, cake or its tidy lunch
menu, to become looser in the evening with
sharing plates and a wide wine and cocktails
selection. The front bis- tro section is also home
to a rich lunch buffet, only to transform into
a bar as the sun sets. Daizy used to be based
across the other side of the mini-district, but has
moved into much more spacious digs. Clearly,
the punters have spoken.
• Daizy, Räffelstrasse 28, Kreis 3, daizy.ch

Food · Shop Red Sea Pedestrians

A third of Swiss Jews live in Zurich, with
Wiedikon home to many Orthodox communities.
A more secular scene is to be found at two
establishments in particular. Stylish *Grand Café
Lochergut* blends Ashkenazi and Sephardi on
its menu—from salmon bagels to shakshuka.
Open breakfast to late night, it also hosts Jewish-
or Israeli-inspired music nights. Around the
corner, Ayal and Judith ply Israeli artifacts and
foodstuffs at *Fein & Dein* (pictured). Honey from
Ayal's father and olives from his uncle feature
alongside vintage pieces and more. Stop by for
a chat or to browse their diverse Hebrew library.
• Kreis 3, various locations, see Index p.63

Happening in the Hood

In a city long-famous for its art scene, the established galleries and newer wave of spaces set up over the last decade are already being added to by a cacophony of younger and more dynamic creative voices. *Kulturfolger* is one such collective, which manifests itself in an annual publication, artistic interventions, and various exhibitions, workshops and talks at its Wiedikon space. The latter might just be the easiest way for a Zurich visitor to access their particular vision of "humans and other civilised animals".
• Kulturfolger, Idastraße 46, Kreis 3,
  kulturfolger.ch

Night | **Emancipate Yourself**

The distressed concrete walls of *Raygrodski* have seen many people drink their own distresses away on a heaving weekend night or a quieter weekday, when the barmen pluck the bottles from their overhead grill with more personalised cocktail advice. The bar's name comes from an early 20th-century women's rights campaigner—look for Paulette's powerful profile on the logo. Her namesake venue makes for an empowering stop en route to or from the other treats in the booming Wiedikon bar scene.
• Raygrodski, Sihlfeldstrasse 49, Kreis 3,
Sihlfeldstrasse 49, raygrodski.ch

Outdoors | **Other World**

Open every day of the year for exploratory walks, existential musings or just some down time, *Friedhof Sihlfield* (Sihlfield Cemetery) is a treasured green space of the city. It's a protected zone, as much for botanical reasons—it's home to more than 70 species of birds, for example—as historical ones. Though the latter is also important, as it was the first civic cemetery in Zurich when it opened in 1877. The gigantic tombs are breathtaking, as is the natural setting that shows the best of each season.
• Friedhof Sihlfield, Aemtlerstrasse 151, Kreis 3

No Concept, Just Taste

As every global city is invaded by leagues of concept stores so perfectly individual they end up seeming the same, it's rare to find somewhere that really embodies a particular and intriguing aesthetic. Perhaps that's why the men behind *Rost und Gold* refuse to use the "c word" about their store. Werner made a name for himself as a flamboyant antiques trader in the 1990s, while Roland worked in theatrical productions and TV casting before their pop-up shop initiative grew wings and put down roots. Now their store hosts a fantastical blend of furniture, lamps and bizarre objects—from baroque to mid-century-design. A cultural programme includes art exhibitions, jazz concerts, readings, parties and plenty more to bring the rust and gold to life. The store is open just Thursday to Saturday: the proprietors, partners in life as well as work, spend the rest of the time searching through Europe for the next piece to add to their collection. Among several other intriguing shops in the area, *Eco Design Home* is notable for its striking and stylish home objects made from sustainable materials. The private showroom is accessible by appointment only.

• Rost und Gold, Uetlibergstrasse 15, Kreis 3, rostundgold.ch; Eco Design Home, Binzstrasse 7, Kreis 3, ecodesignhome.ch

Simon Husslein
He's a product designer whose work extends from super functional watch creation all the way to spatial installation. Having worked closely with Hannes Wettstein, shaping the work of the studio in recent times, he has since opened his own atelier which swings between client brief and personal project

Simon Husslein, Product Designer

Productive View

After time in London, Tokyo and Shanghai, Simon has found his place upon a Zurich hill. Here, he leads a tour through his homeland's uber-sleek design—though he's happy to veer off through a forest and to a restaurant perfect for its imperfections

Since its 2011 founding, Hermann Germann Contemporary has cut a path with its subversive approaches to mixed art

You've lived in London and Shanghai —why settle in Zurich? What makes the city special for you?

I feel very fortunate to live here with my family. Zurich's claim from the 1990s, to be the "Little Big City", sounds arbitrary but I find it a charming description. Here there's a superb quality of life and a great airport nearby. Check out dearzurich.com and fall in love.

Which area of the city do you live in? How is it unique from the rest?

The district is Zürichberg. It's more expensive—not that I have that much to spend—but really nice for families. It's above the city, on the hillside towards the sun. It has good infrastructure and is close to the forest, where we often go with the children. But Zurich is small—on my bike I can be in the centre within

minutes—especially because it's downhill.

Swiss design has a lot to do with typography. What's your favourite font?

After watching the documentary "Helvetica" by Gary Hustwit I felt puzzled: do I actually like the font itself or just the feeling of familiarity I get when seeing it? I guess it's both. Akkurat by the designer Laurenz Brunner is great, too. As is Neuzeit by Wilhelm Pischner.

Where in Zurich can we explore the Swiss approach towards design?

I'd start my tour taking a look at the 25hours Hotel, designed by Alfredo Häberli in his playful and colourful manner. Then I'd visit the *Museum für Gestaltung* next door, they always have great design exhibitions. The museum is inside the Toni Areal—inspiring

The eyes of the founders' role models gaze upon you while you enjoy fine food and a rough-and-ready vibe at Josef

architecture by EM2N and home of Zurich's University of the Arts. From there it's a short walk to the *Freitag Flagship Store* to spot some trucks from the top of the iconic tower made from shipping containers; and then to *Frau Gerolds Garten* for a coffee. Nearby is the *Im Viadukt* mall, which houses a nice mix of objects and furniture, as well as clothing and a food hall. The shops are inside the massive arches of the above train tracks. If you need to cool down afterwards... I love diving into the river Limmat at *Unterer Letten*, at least during summertime.

As a watch designer, what's your favourite public clock in Zurich?
It's not a Zurich exclusive, but it's hard to beat: the Swiss railway clock. An omnipresent archetype of good design.

Where's your inspiration in town?
I like getting lost at *Neumarkt 17*, the most amazing furniture store there is. Everything is nicely curated and decorated inside a maze of subterranean rooms under the Old Town. And I love to sit on the little pier next to the sculpture "Heureka" by Jean Tinguely, at Zürichhorn.

Regarding shopping for art and design products, where are the best places in Zurich to pick up something unique?
You have the well-selected furniture stores at Neumarkt 17 and there's *Teo Jakob*—they have a nice selection of accessories and smaller design objects, in addition to the furniture and the lights they sell. Not far away is *Limited Stock*, a small store by two guys with a really nice selection of limited edition things. If I had to recommend one place, Limited Stock would be it.

For a classic Zurich dinner experience—where would you take us?

Certainly *Kronenhalle*. Iconic for its style, service and their version of "züri-gschnätzlets"—of course alongside "rösti".

And for creative cuisine—any recommendations?

Josef. Preferably on a Friday or Saturday when DJs are playing. I've liked the atmosphere since I first went. It's really positive—not slick or super perfect. In Zurich this is unique because a lot of places look high-end and high-design—made to perfection. At Josef the food is fantastic but also playfully decorated. They have one wall with a huge collage of their heroes. It's a nice way to make a statement. Food-wise, they don't have starters or main dishes. It's more about ordering small plates until you aren't hungry any more. The owners are always looking for new ways, and you can sense this in the guests—they're interesting, not just hungry.

And for drinks after dinner?

After dinner at Kronenhalle go next door to the world-famous Kronenhalle Bar, designed by the Haussmanns. Otherwise I like going to *La Stanza* nearby Paradeplatz, which is also known for good coffee.

If you left town for a short break on Sunday, where would you go?

With family, I'd take the Dolderbahn train to the restaurant *Wirtschaft Degenried*, followed by a stroll in the forest. With friends, to *Teehütte Fallätsche* up the Üetliberg mountain by train, followed by a walk over the hill top. With a vintage Porsche 944, to *Restaurant Neuhof* in Bachs, a short ride through the northern suburbs. There are weird places here where you don't feel near a city. You quickly find yourself in a remote environment that could be

the last valley—but you're still close to the airport so there are planes right over. It's a fun combination.

Are there any museums or galleries we shouldn't miss?

Besides super-duper *Löwenbräukunst* and *Kunsthaus*, check what's on at *Helmhaus*, which is always good for surprises. I remember amazing exhibitions like Max Bill and James Turrell at *Museum Haus Konstruktiv*.

Are there any young talents from town on your watch list?

Check the lineup at *Herrmann Germann Contemporary*—old friends of mine started it. They're looking to exhibit interesting people, not just from Switzerland. The selection is hard to describe: I don't know exactly what they're looking for, I just know that if they have a show it feels special. It's a bit disturbing maybe, a bit weird, but always high quality. You always have to position yourself within the pieces and explore what you think and why. It's a sign of quality in contemporary art, if you have to search for your opinion. They're not a super fancy or famous gallery yet so they had to find a niche. If you're looking for young talent, find it there.

If you could redesign a classic Swiss product, what would it be?

When eating delicious "luxemburgerli"—an airy dessert like a smaller, lighter macaron—from *Confiserie Sprüngli*, I always wonder why they look like tiny hamburgers that Pantone could have used as samples to present their latest selection. It would be fun changing their shape, since they already inspire colour selection for products during my design meetings.

Photo: Frau Gerolds Garten

Get amongst the urban gardening scene at Frau Gerolds Garten, at the foot of the Freitag Tower

Dirt, Spirit and Soul

Diving beneath the Zurich veneer

Thomas Haemmerli

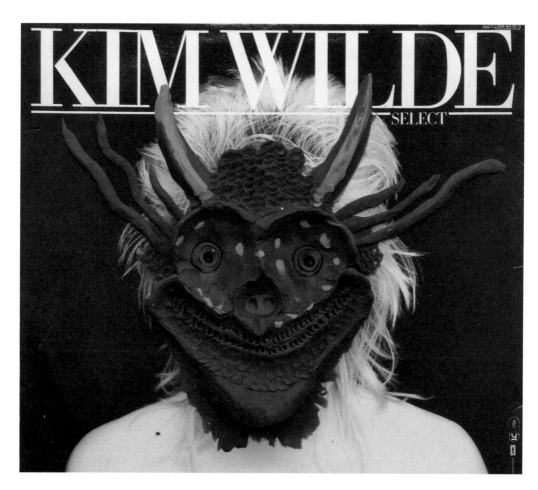

Small sculptures of empty cans and vodka bottles decorate the side-walk. Often you can guess what some teenager ate before he tested his holding capacity's limits. At the corner shop on Langstrasse/ Stauffacher, early-bird alcoholics hang next to late clubbers with a beer. Where I live, do not expect Swiss cleanliness—on the contrary.

It is early Sunday morning and I'm off to Bank, a former branch of a big financial institute that now houses a hip café. "Morning Mr. Director" I shout to Yves who stands behind a counter. Yves blinks ironically. It's still a bit strange to meet in the early hours. Yves was once king of Zurich's nightlife. His illegal parties were a must. These days he's an entrepreneur. Yves i^s one of several guys who defied Zurich's once rigid system of gastronomy with illegal bars. In the 1980s, Zurich was constricted by the "necessity clause": per so many heads, only one restaurant was permitted. With few exceptions everything had to close by midnight. So young rebels bought alcohol, put a plank on beer crates and handed out flyers for their pop-up bars. Small cellars developed into chic venues like multi-floored Kurtz, or Cinque, where you needed a credit card to open the door.

The other factor that changed Zurich's face forever was "Don Raffaele". Doctor Raphael Huber was the chief official responsible for allowing a bar to lengthen its counter by 70cm, or to stay open until 2am. In quiet Zurich that was worth millions. Huber liked to say: "I have expenses!" Anyone who wanted his help had to pay stiff prices for paintings by Pietri Corsen, nom de plume of Huber's untalented father Adolph. When the scandal broke the bribes had been invested in Huber's Tuscan vineyards. He did some years inside. But a large part of the money never surfaced—il Dottore had married his Italian housekeeper who received the estate, while he kept the dog, Nero. And the housekeeper, of course.

Goodbye Zwingli

Both Don Raffaele and the illegal bars led to a wide liberalisation of Zurich's nightlife, turning the austere Protestant city so upside down that philosopher Georg Kohler coined the term "mediterranisation". These days, fewer than half its inhabitants are Protestant. Immigration from Catholic cantons, an influx of Italians and Baltic refugees changed the mix. And though I'm talking about religion, I'm not referring to actual believers; rather to patterns of mentality. I'm a good example. I come from a traditional family, where we never went to church and everybody was an atheist. Still, my upbringing was embedded with Protestantism, moulding me so that—put simply—work is paramount and showing feelings is not the done thing. When in the late 1990s head of police Esther Maurer tried to bring closing times back, I designed the campaign against her, depicting Maurer as a sour Zwinglian. (If you talk about Zurich, don't mention Calvinism. Calvin is Geneva. We had our own Protestant reformer: Huldrych Zwingli.) It worked.

Concrete vs. Dada

Zwingli also lives on in the Zurich school of concrete and constructive art: rational, geometrical, sober and reduced. In short, it fits Zurich. Dadaism, the town's other, far more influential art movement had—until recently— only low esteem from official Zurich. The anarchic anti-war art movement started by Hugo Ball in 1916 was always seen as foreign. Because of its nonsensical playful character. Because Dada's loud aggression to authority was too shrill for Zurich's unwritten imperative of moderation. But foremost because the Dadaists were all foreigners, refugees from World War I. Their contemporary—local writer and honest Social-Democrat Charlot Strasser— wrote the novel "Vermin around the Lantern", describing Dadaists as shady spies, profiteers and druggies. And it was true. Emmy Hennings, Ball's companion, was a part-time prostitute who loved morphine as much as Ball himself, who narrated their outsider existence in his semi-autobiographical novel "Flametti, or the Dandyism of the poor". But more recently, Dada profited from a hoax.

The ghost pharmacy

Mark Divo is a slick bastard: manipulator, curator, artist, activist. A silver-back among Zurich squatters. And the organiser of Dada Week, where he invites artist friends from all over Europe. From his days in Germany, Divo learned you can't beat the system militarily. His conclusion: public relations. Meaning, find allies and have demands beyond your usual punk concert. In 2002 a big company acquired the house on Spiegelgasse where the Dadaists' Cabaret Voltaire had started with Lenin living just around the corner. Divo squatted the building, demanding the birthplace of Dada be preserved. He put it out that a pharmacy was to be opened there. A pure lie—but a clever one. Some years earlier, young intellectuals had campaigned to reunite the famous Café Odeon, former hangout of the literati. It's currently divided like Cold War Germany. One half remains a café, while the other is a pharmacy. With no official statements about the future of Cabaret Voltaire, an outcry broke out: "Dada's cultural heritage will be desecrated again! By another pharmacy!" The call was taken up by the papers. Then Swatch boss Nicolaus Hayek, who has a weakness for crazy projects, called the mayor. In short, Divo's lie resulted in "Dada Haus Cabaret Voltaire", a cultural institution paid for by the city. And though the renovation gave it the look and feel of an evangelical youth cellar, they do have quite good events from time to time.

Art foundations

Zurich is a centre for contemporary art for three reasons. First, as a Protestant city, the old elites were restrained and sober. It was bad taste to show off. In a popular anecdote, Russian oligarch Viktor Vekselberg visited the home of Zurich's most powerful lawyer. The house was typical of the old bourgeois area of Zürichberg—spacious but not huge. As legend has it, Vekselberg said: "You call this a house? I call this a hut." In Russia you show what you have. Not in Zurich. But art is the one exception. Preferably contemporary: it requires knowledge to buy correctly and is understandable only for the cognoscenti—not the nouveaux riche.

Second, the rest of the continent was ruptured by World War II, when the Nazis destroyed or confiscated the art. Switzerland was still buying. Among

Old Money it's not uncommon to have had three generations of collectors. And third: though Switzerland might no longer be the first choice for dictators and mafia bosses, Swiss banks are still a fine place to hide funds. But as pressure on black money increases, art provides an alternative. Sure, there are now anti-money laundering rules for art dealers. But for enough cash, you can still get very good art (though perhaps none by Pietri Corsens). One more story. In 2002, Art Basel, the world's most important art fair, opened in Miami, with the main sponsor Zurich's big bank UBS. Years later a whistleblower revealed how UBS advisors went to Miami like mini James Bonds. Their laptops had two operating systems and a panic button to erase the banking part. At the fanciest art parties, they convinced rich collectors to stash money in Switzerland. It must be said that Swiss banks now try to avoid untaxed money. At least from clients in the US or EU. And while in the 1980s and 1990s you often found yourself dancing in former factories, all of a sudden empty spaces are popping up in abandoned vaults. Jobs in banking, once good for a lifetime, aren't safe anymore. The new big thing now is to park money in expensive art you then store in the freeports of Geneva or Zurich. "Uber-warehouses for the ultra-rich", announced "The Economist".

Holy grail of the underground

Zurich's posh gallery hotspot is the Löwenbräu complex, also home to art book publishers JRP Ringier and Patrick Frey. If the right people in the city think you're good, you can have a sensational career. You'll get into a world-class gallery like Eva Presenhuber or Hauser & Wirth, "Parkett" magazine will write a eulogy, JRP will publish the book and you're made. You'll see great art in Zurich, and the right attitude—blasé self-entitlement —might get you an invite to the vernissage afterparty.

Otherwise try the off-scene or the squats, good for ending up in one of the few remaining illegal bars or hidden restaurants. But they appear only from time to time, and everybody shuddered when they heard of someone who had to pay 50,000 dollars fine for his pop-up restaurant. In the good old days this would have got him at least one Pietri Corsen painting. But if you can't find the holy grail of Zürich's underground just try Langstraße where I live, and where you have everything... Drunken locals, drunken tourists, drunken idiots, the few remaining street hookers and puking teenagers. And if you stay out long enough, you'll see me on my way to Yves kicking cans out of the way, mumbling maledictions about what the fuck happened to this city and why can't we have some order and strict closing times for Christ's sake.

Thomas Haemmerli is a documentary director, an author and a political activist. As his home town Zürich seems far too small, he lives as well in his homes in São Paulo, Tbilisi and Mexico City. Consequently his next film is called "I am Gentrification—Confessions of a Scoundrel"

Photo: An original piece by Beni Bischof, that hangs on the wall of good Protestant Thomas Haemmerli

Fashion and Finance

Marc & Helena Bernegger
Helena was born in Berlin, grew up in in London and studied in Amsterdam, a background that laid foundations for a fascination with new trends, and her own style consultancy Fashion Fräulein. Zurich-born Marc has been called one of Europe's most influential technology investors. He set up a successful nightlife platform at just 20 years old, founded several other web companies afterwards and he remains highly active in the European fintech scene

Zurich is a fondue of international and local professionals at the top of their game. That's where we find Marc and Helena, who share their roadmaps to the favourite haunts of financiers and fashionistas

Suppose you have visitors, where would you go?

Helena: From our neighbourhood Römerhof, we'd take the Dolder Bahn up the hill for a walk through the forest. En route we'd enjoy a great city view at Sonnenberg and have coffee and cake at the organic grocer *Justus*. Then we'd go downtown to *Kunsthaus Zürich* and walk through the Old Town. A quick lunch at *Terrasse* and a walk down Bahnhofstrasse towards the lake. At night we'd dine at *Lumière* and go for cocktails at *Widder Bar*.

Helena, you are originally from Berlin—how does Zurich compare?

Helena: Zurich and Berlin are like Yin and Yang. Zurich is a small, safe and clean city where everything is organised and people are polite. I feel that living between both cities is the best you can get.

You have a child—what do you do on the weekends?

Helena: Soon we'll have two! We often go to the Dolder forest, Artergut Playground, or for a boat trip on the lake.

Imagine the grandparents are babysitting. Where would you go?

Helena: We use free evenings to test out new restaurants. Among others, *Kornsilo* at Mühle Tiefernbrunnen, *Grand Café Lochergut* for an easy dinner or *Bank*.

Helena, you're a style consultant. What's the Zurich style code?

Helena: I would underdress rather than overdress. The Swiss are not very loud or fancy in fashion, compared to other countries. Go for a nice pair of body-hugging jeans, loafers and a cashmere sweater or blouse. For men it's similar—classic fits best.

Where to get such an outfit here?

Helena: All big brands and stores are on Bahnhofstrasse. For unique and selected items try *Modestrom* for fashion with a fancy taste, *Vestibules* for international designers, and *Monadico* for accessories. These shops are on Seefeldstrasse. For men, try local brand *Pelikamo*.

What are the hot names for original Zurich designs?

Helena: *Townhouse* is a concept store that sells fashion, art, beauty products and much more. *EnSoie* started off with ceramics and is very popular nowadays for fashion and accessories. *Little Black Dress* is a design duo who create beautiful dresses for women.

Marc, where can we taste Zurich's financial metropolis?

Marc: The Paradeplatz area, where UBS and Credit Suisse have their HQ, along with most private banks. For lunch, try *Tao's* for new Asian or *Bärengasse* for a great steak. For drinks, *La Stanza* or *Lima*.

Where would you go for lunch to celebrate a deal?

Depending on budget a lunch at one of the restaurants of five-star hotel Baur au Lac: *Rive Gauche* or *Pavillon*. There's a nice terrace for summertime.

You're also involved in the art world—any recommendations?

Marc: You'll find a lot of interesting and international galleries in Kreis 5. One favourite is *Karma International*. And check out art gallery *Scheublein + Bak* inside the Sihlberg castle.

Laura de Weck, Performer & Playwright

Cultural Commuter

Laura de Weck
She grew up in Paris, Hamburg, and Zurich, where she graduated from drama school. After her 78-year-old mentor persuaded her to start writing, her debut play was a hit that performed in eight theatres. Since then she has forged a name for herself Europe-wide as an actress, director and author, with pieces translated into several languages

Presenting a city of luxury prostitution, wild contemporary dance and delicious slices of veal in white wine and cream is Laura, whose dramatic eye and poetic sensibility discover the pleasant roughness behind Zurich's shiny façade

What do you like best about Zurich? What do you think could be better?

Zurich is extraordinarily beautiful and above all very clean. But sometimes it's too clean—too perfectly styled. It lacks untidy corners, improvisation, and things that are still a work in progress. In that respect Zurich could do better by being a bit more relaxed.

What do you do on the weekend?

I like the bars, the small ones in Kreis 4 like *Bar 63, Total Bar, Olé-Olé-Bar*, and the special, upmarket places like *Kronenhalle*. *Tina Bar* in the Old Town even allows smoking. And don't forget *Meyer's*—one of the few bars that stays open into the early hours.

Where's good for a meal with friends?

Restaurants in Zurich are expensive, and always full—but they're very good! The Italian places *Ristorante Italia* and *Morgenstern* are amazing; for a snack, *Palestine Grill* is very good. In *Zum Goldenen Fass* you can have pimped-up retro Swiss food, and in *Rechberg* you sit at large, family-size tables and eat seasonal and regional dishes.

Where is the best cheese fondue?

People often say the most authentic fondue mixture is at the Co-op supermarket. You can also order a super one at *Fribourger Fonduestübli*.

Where do you take your Hamburg friends on their second visit?

To the "badis" (swimming baths) of course, because we haven't been to all of them yet. And there's a secret baroque garden near Neumarkt tram station—*Rechberg*.

Do people still dance in Zurich?

Sure, but they need a little alcohol before their hips start to move. That's why dancing tends to start rather late. The Stadt-sommerkonzerte ("city summer concerts") include appearances all over the town from the younger Swiss music scene. There is also *Club Zukunft* for an electric vibe and *Helsinkiklub* to dance to hand-picked, alternative bands.

What is your favourite spot?

I am fond of the square in front of Bahnhof Stadelhofen. I spent all my time there when I was young. It used to have benches. From there, the station overpass looks like a whale skeleton, although the architect, Calatrava, apparently modelled it on a bull's ribs. And for a lovely place to relax, drink coffee and maybe let the kids run around, go to quiet Hallwylplatz.

What type of culture best represents the spirit of Zurich?

Of course I love the theatre. The smaller theatres are especially close to the current reality of Zurich life. Go to *Theaterhaus Gessnerallee*, where there's wild, contemporary dance, theatre, and even performances for non-German speakers.

Dada—another fixed point on the tourist trail. Does it still exist?

In the *Cabaret Voltaire* on Spiegelgasse, of course. I also performed there quite recently.

If you wrote a play about Zurich—who would be the main characters?

A few years ago there was a famous article about luxury prostitution here. It covered everything that makes Zurich what it is: wealth, decadence, dirt, forbidden things, double standards, desire, wildness, sadness and dreams. I'd have a clever young sex worker as main character and, as a contrast, another young woman who's a rather reserved student.

Spectral Scenes

Douglas Mandry

The Zurich-based artist's work responds to the soulless landscape of digitalisation with physically reworked analogue prints. Like a fantastical version of classic Swiss mountain photography, Douglas transforms the traditional into something otherworldly

Kalabrese
He came up during wilder times in Zurich, first as a drummer for hip hop band Sendak before becoming a DJ and producer. He helped found the award-winning Club Zukunft over ten years ago and has since transformed it into the city's most important dance music venue

Kalabrese, Musician

Free as a Child

Sacha Winkler has been a contributing member of Zurich's clubbing scene for decades. Ahead, we learn how to begin, end and recover from a perfect night in the city, with or without your mother

Excellent, simple and reasonably priced food revolves around the grill at Gamper Restaurant

You've been running one of Zurich's most prominent nightclubs for over ten years and your history as a musician and DJ goes farther back… What was the city like when you set out?

My socialisation process began as a teenager when I spent time in a youth centre in Zurich near the lake. I was involved in things like organising concerts and cinema-nights. I also had a rehearsal room there where we'd jam with other musicians. We weren't on a high level technically, but we were motivated and shared a feeling. When I stopped with football, music became the centre of my activities. After this my mother sent me to a drum teacher to learn more, and I'm very blessed for that. Zurich did have a bigger alternative scene than now. There were more people doing things without a commercial goal. But maybe it's that when you

become an adult you start to opti-mise your activities to earn more money—I don't know. For sure we had more space and time then; ex-industrial zones with large spaces for cultural activities. With gentrification we lost our freedom, but we're all part of this develop-ment. It's tragic, but at the same time it represents a chance to move on.

How has Zurich affected your music? Is it present in your creative output?

My mother took me to jazz and other concerts. She's very open-minded and has been a real influence on my musical career. She's been following my music for years and we communicate easily. I would listen to my parents' records early on—Hendrix, The Doors, Miles Davis, Frank Zappa—then spend the whole night under my pillow listening to radio stations

Zurich's legendary venue Rote Fabrik was established in an old silk mill after a massive popular campaign

from all over the world. In the 1990s I became part of a sub-cultural scene through my ex-girl-friend. I started spinning records for a techno crowd. I played a funny mix with kickin' electronica, James Brown, deep house and techno. I was influenced a lot by other DJs and producers like Bang Goes or Styro 2000. As a musician I was interested in jamming and improvisation. In techno, only those guys could do it with machines.

There's a widespread notion that the Swiss are prim and proper, that everything is perfect... What could we see in Zurich to dispel this idea?

Just take bus number 32 after work, go down Langstraße and you'll have a melting pot: druggies with dogs in a restless mood but always with a sense of humour, nightlife kids with bottles of alcohol

and older people from proper areas all come together on a bus.

Receiving international artists every weekend must have turned you into a city ambassador—where do you take people when they visit?

In the summer I bring them to the river. At *Oberen Letten* there's a swim area and a lovely place for having an aperitivo, *Panama*. In the winter I prefer museums —*Kunst-haus* and *Löwenbräu*—or to spend time in a café. My favourites are *Sport Bar* and *Café Noir*, two very intimate places perfect for freelance people to work and network.

Can you tell us some of your favourite spots for a dinner before a big night?

The Zukunft team regularly visits an Italian restaurant called *Morgenstern*. Mario is the owner, a very charismatic person who knows how to celebrate life and party too. We usually have a separate room for ourselves and he also lets us come late and eat spontaneously. There is a new one near *Club Zukunft* called *Gamper*. They're young cooks who bring fresh food and simple recipes to the table—I prefer it simple. If we have enough time and budget, a classy spot is *Kronenhalle*, a Zurich institution. A must if you want to try the famous "Züri Gschnätzlets".

Where can we buys records in Zurich?
A couple of months ago I discovered the new assortment at OOR Records. One of the owners has a great taste for independent music, from weird electronic stuff to nu-disco, afro, techno and other styles. For secondhand visit *16tons* or *Zero Zero Rare Groove*, they have a huge collection. It's music history for sure: if you want to become a real connoisseur, spend time there and talk to the owner or set aside a day to dig.

No clubbing tonight—where should we get some drinks?
Most of the time I prefer my home, watching movies, reading the news or inviting friends for dinner. Though sometimes I go out for a drink and an intimate conversation. I like classic bars. *Old Crow* in the lovely Old Town is amazing. Near my club you have *Bar 63*. They have all sorts of rum and it's a place to easily start a conversation with a stranger. At the end of the night you'll realise that Zurich is a village, not a city—everyone knows someone you know.

Or if we wanted to hear some great live music?
Moods is a good jazz club; *El Lokal* is also perfect for alternative music, or *Rote Fabrik*. *Kaufleuten* has the most beautiful concert space, I had my record release

concert there with my eight-piece orchestra. It was amazing. The room is classy and all in wood.

During winter, where can you go to escape from all the nightlife?
The mountains are close enough, with really quiet places to escape to. I prefer the region of Engadin, especially Unterengadin, with the villages of Guarda and Val Mustair. When you catch a nice sunny autumn day, you must go there; you will find one of the greatest views and a colourful plant festival.

Are there any mountain cafés or refuges where we could have a drink up high?
For a perfect fondue you can go to restaurant *Wirtschaft Degenried*, near the Dolder hotel. Afterwards, for a nice walk and a coffee or dessert, the *Restaurant Die Waid*.

You spend a lot of nights in Zukunft: how do you nurse your hangover?
At home or going out for a walk. Sometimes I start Mondays with a longer brunch with my mother or a good friend. *Grand Café Lochergut* opened recently. They have really good mezze—perfect for sharing. And I love the *Volkshaus*, it's a perfect place to start your day alone. You can bring your laptop, because others do the same, and if you find buddies you can extend your stay for dinner.

Zurich has such a particular cultural history—how's the arts scene these days?
Even if we are known for being the financial city we still have a lively cultural scene with an impressive output. I really love theatre and modern dance, like Christoph Marthaler's absurd theater and the classical speech-oriented work of Barbara Frey. Both are very poetic. My old band buddy

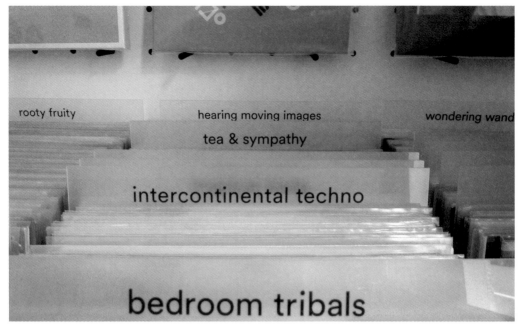

rooty fruity

hearing moving images

wondering wand

tea & sympathy

intercontinental techno

bedroom tribals

Allow yourself some time to get lost in the unique musical taste of the owner at OOR Records

Spa at
The Dolder Grand
Kreis 7

Seebad Enge
Kreis 2

Dimitri is one half of Zimmermann & de Perrot; they're quirky and funky with a perfect mélange of dance, slapstick humor and art. Sidi Larbi Cherkaoui is one of the freshest choreographers, dancers and musicians—and a real bridge builder for me.

What's your favourite summer terrace and cosy winter hangout?
I prefer the hills along the Waid. You can walk there and have a fantastic overview. But most of the time I just look out my window. It's my first flat with such a great view—I live on a hill by Goldbrunnen. In winter I start my fire and read a book, or invite friends for a long talk with red wine. For wellness, I like to go to the *Spa at The Dolder Grand*. Or the sauna at *Seebad Enge*. It's an outdoor sauna right upon the lake.

What do you miss most about Zurich when you're abroad?
Nothing. Because when I see a new city, I check out the vibe. That's always exciting. Even if I visit a city repeatedly.

Is there any place in Zurich we would never find you?
No, I'm a curious person.

What's the perfect soundtrack for getting lost in Zurich?
I wrote a song with the name "Sihltal" in Swiss German and later an English song called "Kafi Lied". Both represent that feeling you have as an artist living in a small town with bigger dreams. The relationship with the city is one of pain and satisfaction. It's about finding a balance between structural life and the space to be as free as a child.

Over the Tracks

While gentrification waits around the corner, this area, formerly notorious for heroin and prostitution, still retains enough of its seamy dark side to remain interesting

| Night | Long and Winding Road |

Nocturnal explorers have ground to cover along Zurich's entertainment artery Langstraße. On its most eccentric corner, *Olé-Olé-Bar* is cloaked in an unassuming red-brick building. Within, find a cranky jukebox, intense décor and the saviour of many a broke boozer: the "Johnny Cash Machine". At the heart of the former red light district, ex-cabaret venue *Longstreet* (pictured) hosts an eclectic range of quality parties. A staple in the local diet is next door: *Palestine Grill*, with friendly vendors, and delicacies for carnivores and veggies alike. A fine next stop, *Gonzo*, is just a stroll away. You might not spot the entrance, but follow the queue—it leads to distorted guitars and more "mexikaner" shots than you can handle. When you're done, fritter your last francs on some doughy consolation at *Happy Bäckerei*, open 24 hours to all—no matter their state.

• Kreis 4, various locations, see Index p.62

Tour de Zurich

Meat hangs from above and the beer flows freely at *Les Halles*, a jolly market-bar-restaurant hybrid where you can buy anything from a bicycle to a sausage. Order at the counter and be prepared for the decibel levels to rise with each passing hour. The menu, a paper slip on which to mark your preferences, has an uncontested star— the moules frites. Alternatively, take your pick from the deli counter's meats and bring it back to your checkered tablecloth, where you might be seated beside a group of businessmen or beer quaffing retirees.
• Les Halles, Pfingstweidstrasse 6, Kreis 5, les-halles.ch

Food | **Mane Meal**

It might look like an old-school diner in a train station, but *Eisenhof* is a legendary stop owing to another retro form of transport. Namely, horse. A juicy 250g filet of horsemeat is the specialty at this unpretentious joint bang in the middle of Zurich's trendzone. Though beef and cordon bleu are also offered, the sheer tastiness of the equine option is guaranteed to dissolve all moral scruples. Served rare on hot stones—so you can continue to cook it as you please—the steak draws in a crowd of faithful old timers along with an increasing percentage of youngsters too.
• Restaurant Eisenhof, Gasometerstrasse 20, Kreis 5, restauranteisenhof.ch

Food | **Check Please**

Once headquarters to Credit Suisse, this café and restaurant makes no attempt to hide its former identity. But you won't find Gordon Gekko here— Bank has a policy of equality that means all its employees are well paid and respected. Not to mention an affordable, organic menu. Drop in for breakfast, but be ready to wait for a seat in the sun. Decked out in muted pinks and the smell of freshly-baked bread, indoor seating—with dozens of tables to choose from—is not a bad alternative. The music is kept low to facilitate conversation— just what we like with our Sunday coffee.
• Bank, Molkenstrasse 15, Kreis 4, bankzuerich.ch

Thought Catalogue

Though it rides under the banner of a sustainable, ecological concept store, *Soeder* is more than just an exercise in marketing buzzwords. The range and quality of the products stocked will allow you to renovate your lifestyle piece by piece. Books and art, kitchenware, organic makeup and even a simple, earthy selection of clothing for women, men and children will all keep you busy for a while. Everything is sourced from Switzerland or Europe and though it might not be the place to bargain hunt, the goods are built to last.
• Soeder, Ankerstraße 124, Kreis 4, soeder.ch

Shop · Food   **The Mallness of it All**

Thanks to architectural crimes around the world, shopping malls are forever off-putting to the sophisticated shopper. Yet, fitted nicely under a railway overpass as it is, *Im Viadukt* gives all the perks of a high-end mall without the exhausting-claustrophobia. Meaning enough energy to peruse its curated shops, such as concept store *Cabinet*, a pick among the many interior design locales. But there are more than a dozen fashion retailers too, and because there's more to life than dresses and drawers, the food stalls of *Markthalle* will nourish another side of you.
• Im Viadukt, Viaduktstraße, Kreis 5, im-viadukt.ch

Food   **Black Gold**

Every city has an assortment of places claiming "the best coffee in town"—but the blend at *Café Noir* is served up in bars all over Zurich, so there might be something to it. Since opening in 2006 with an authentic 1960s coffee roaster and a Dalla Corte espresso machine, it's become a star in the city's coffeescape. Varieties are available separately as well as blended, and sold to take away—whole, hand- or electric-ground. Parts for various coffee machines are stocked, showing they mean business. And the tiny, stylish interior is perfect for observing the particular crowd coming through.
• Café Noir, Neugasse 33, Kreis 5, cafe-noir.ch

Industrial without so much chic—*Rosso* is hidden in a converted warehouse with no sign outside to direct you in. Book or face a fair wait for a place at the shared tables—and then bask in pizza paradise. From the paper-thin crust to the sauce, the pies are made from scratch and with love. They're served by staff adept at navigating the large, rowdy groups of diners that fill the huge space up after dusk. Lunchtime is a slightly quieter affair, and it's good to remember the alternatives: the antipasti dishes are just as satisfying.
• Rosso, Geroldstrasse 31, Kreis 5, restaurant-rosso.ch

Food | Baccanal

Though it might be Michelin-rated, *Caduff's* doesn't take itself too seriously. It is definitely a white-glove experience, but guests are encouraged to wander down into a cavernous, candle-lit wine cellar to choose any bottle they please—with friendly assistance, should they need it. Cheese is also handled on a choose-your-own-adventure basis, serving as a fun prelude to whatever compact, seasonal wonders the menu may hold. And if you're lucky, that wine cellar tour might even be given by Beat Caduff himself.
• Caduff's Wine Loft, Kanzleistrasse 126, Kreis 4, wineloft.ch

Shop | Cutting-edge Cuts

If you think Zürchers are conservative dressers, check out the racks of these shops. Bearing avant-garde tastes and unexpected silhouettes, they might well pull you out your comfort zone. At minimalistic and experimental *Berenik* (Kreis 5), find clothes and stand-out accessories made from quality materials with comfort and endurance in mind. A cruise through *Waldraud* (Kreis 5), meanwhile, might resemble a gallery visit, complete with neon cushions and one-off leather goods. The passionate and patient assistants will happily guide you to your next little treasure.
• Various locations, see Index p.62 for details

Secret Ingredient

Alex Kühn
He had his nose in the Michelin and Gault Millau guides at ten years old, but his studies pushed him into sports journalism. Finally after years of reviewing restaurants on the side, Alex was offered the position of food writer at his newspaper "Tages-Anzeiger"— and his palate has never been happier

Standing at the crossroads of France, Germany and Italy, Switzerland is a culinary crucible—but high prices and conservative kitchens mean it's worth having an insider give you some tips. Alex serves up a dish for every occasion

Alex, what's good and bad about the state of dining in Zurich?

It's hard to find a really bad place in Zurich. Probably 90% of restaurants will serve you food that's at least reasonable. The bad thing is that it's not the cheapest, obviously. Also, I think some more creative and experimental restaurants are needed. Here, when you have a creative idea, it's hard to get money, and to build a restaurant in Zurich you need a lot. It's not like in other cities where you just open a place; here you need all the technical things to be perfect to get a license. So it's hard for creative people. The business side is so tricky, you have to be sure it's really going to work—so some people are too conservative.

Where's best for genuine Swiss food?

Zeughauskeller. It's not expensive, you get sausage with potato salad at a reasonable price. It's touristy but good. *Zum Kropf* belongs to the same people, but it's the nobler version. It's a little more expensive and they have a nice terrace. They do good schnitzel, good soups, very good rösti. I'd rather go there than Kronnenhalle, which is too posh and too expensive. And in its bar I don't really like the drinks, they're too sweet and old-fashioned. The barman was world champion in the 1980s and nobody dares to say anything to him now. But there's one very good thing about Kronnenhalle that not a lot of people know about. There's a little room where you can smoke upstairs; only about six people fit in there. There's a telephone there: if you pick it up and dial 911, a waiter will come to serve you.

What's the top cuisine option, regardless of price?

Ecco at the Hotel Atlantis by Giardino is the best. *The Restaurant at the Dolder Grand* is also very good, but Ecco is fresher, more understandable, not as complicated. They have a similar concept at the Ecco restaurants in the canton of Ticino and in the mountains near St. Moritz. Their former sous-chef, Stefan Heilemann, is now chef de cuisine at Ecco in Zurich—he's brilliant, and so is his patissier André Siedl. *EquiTable* with young Swiss chef Fabian Fuchs is also very good: ecologically driven, responsible fine dining.

And what about excellent food at a more affordable level?

Gustav is rather a classic, but still amazing, and the prices are reasonable for what it is. Chef Antonio Colaianni was head chef at the formerly Michelin-starred Mesa and is now at Gustav doing Italian cuisine with a modern twist. It's kind of soul food—classic, but it makes you feel very comfortable.

And for real budget dining?

Metzg at Langstrasse. Their main focus is meat. It's not expensive and it's very, very good. For traditional Italian food in a very cosy environment, try *Pergola*. It's old-fashioned, but you'll feel very comfortable and the food is great. Try the "scaloppine al limone", and eat them with risotto. It's not how you do it but I like it that way.

How about for a down-to-earth traditional experience?

One very simple place is *Restaurant Bahnhof Wiedikon*. You eat for about 20 francs there. It's not fancy food, it's old-fashioned Swiss fare like schnitzel with fries and a salad. I go there a lot. There's a Sri Lankan waiter, who for me is the best waiter in town. He's very quick, remembers everything, knows all my preferences… Some would say it's too old fashioned, but

I like it. It's a very sweet thing; it's one of the last old-school places in these urban areas, so I'd recommend it because it's the real Zurich somehow.

Zurich is a mesh of cultures… Has that resulted in interesting fusions?

It's not in the city but a little outside, in the Kameha Grand Hotel—try *You*, for Japanese-European fusion. The chef Norman Fischer used to work with German three-star chef Christian Bau. You is expensive, but it has one star and Fischer is doing interesting work.

Are there any maverick chefs doing original stuff in the city?

Marius Frehner at *Gamper*, where everything's based around the grill. It's very small but they do really tasty things, like whole grilled leek. It's a great concept and very economical.

Where would you go for a good cocktail in a nice environment?

Tales Bar near Bahnhof Selnau. The owner Wolfgang Bogner used to run the Hyatt's Onyx Bar. But he's developed his own taste now. They're open until 3am, and all the people from other restaurants and bars go when they finish. Try the cocktail with basil and cucumber. Another place is *Rooftop*, on top of the Modissa building. The bartender Jennifer Hunziker is great. She does her own syrups, bitters and shrubs. It's a bit more experimental than Tales. Then you have the classics like *Widder Bar* and *Old Crow*.

And the best cup of Joe?

Milchbar. It's in two buildings, but pick the left-hand one—that's the café. They have a very good barista there with all sorts of coffee.

Is there a non-cheesy way to do fondue?

You can buy a fondue at a shop called *Welschland*, they have a cheese mixture that's supposed to be the best. And if you want to go to a restaurant for fondue I'd probably go to *Le Dézaley*. But fondue is always touristy because Zurich doesn't have that tradition. We'd rather have fried fish from the lake with potatoes and a glass of wine.

Sounds good… Where can we get that?

The best place is 20 minutes outside the city in Stäfa, it's called *Gasthof zur Sonne*. All their fresh-water fish is from Lake Zurich—try the "gebackener hecht" (baked pike) or "eglifilets im bierteig" (perch in beer batter).

What was the most fun review you've written in the last year?

We went to one place that was really bad. They had a dessert called "red velvet cubes". As you can expect it was horrible. I was laughing at my own naïvity—for even ordering it in the first place!

What's your dream for the future of Zurich restaurants?

That each restaurant would have just five or six dishes—but they'd do them very well. They would know the history of the dish, they'd know the guys producing the material and wouldn't try to do fancy stuff… They'd just concentrate on doing good, simple food.

And finally, when in Zurich, drink like the Zürchers… But what?

White wine, specifically Räuschling R3 by Schwarzenbach Weinbau or Riesling—the Madeleine Royale AOC Zürichsee by Lüthi Weinbau.

Above: Expect luxurious surroundings to match the picturesque dishes at You in the Kameha Grand Hotel
Below: Despite the elaborate décor, an unpretentious feel reigns at Zur Kropf—with dishes as Swiss as they come

Chuchichäschtli

Fly Pig

This copper origami is a celebration of metamorphosis. Conceived and made in Switzerland, the metallic porker is a cute reminder that not everything needs a purpose. How Dada.
• Schweini, Strala Gallery, strala.ch

The Wheel Deal

Got a few kilos to spare in that bag? Pick up a wheel of Gruyére, created by master cheesemaker Marc-Henri Horner using traditional methods. If it's too much to handle, Welschland—specialists in Franco-Swiss delicacies—have plenty of lighter alternatives.
• Gruyère, Welschland, welschland.com

Time Piece

Switzerland, the watch aficionado's paradise—except for in Zurich, that is. That's where Maurice de Mauriac, the first brand local to the city, comes in. Pick up a piece of local precision and start a conversation with a fellow time keeper.
• L1, Maurice de Muariac, mauricedemauriac.ch

Books

The Pledge
● Friedrich Dürrenmatt, 1958

A detective promises a bereaved mother he'll catch her daughter's killer. The giant of Swiss postwar drama and literature turned his critical lens onto the genre with this novel.

Gantenbein
● Max Frisch, 1982

Also published with the English title "A Wilderness of Mirrors", this bewildering story by the postmodern maestro explores his favourite theme of identity with a sea of shifting narrators and storylines.

Flight Out of Time: A Dada Diary
● Hugo Ball, John Elderfield

Read the mind-opening memoirs of a key influence in avant-garde art movement Dada, published in English along with related texts. Ball founded Zurich's legendary Cabaret Voltaire, which became a hub for Dada's poetic, philosophical and theatrical side.

Films

Die Schweizermacher
● Rolf Lyssy, 1978

The highest grossing film in Switzerland for nearly 20 years, this satirical comedy follows a disparate group as they try to survive the investigations of a dastardly immigration official and obtain the hallowed Swiss passport.

Electroboy
● Marcel Gisler, 2014

Florian Burkhardt, aka Electroboy, has an impressive resume, from model and snowboard promoter, to author and party promoter. But this documentary about him shows that perceived success is not so simple, and paints a picture of anxiety and human complexity.

The Circle
● Stefan Haupt, 2014

A true story out of mid-20th century Zurich is depicted as a key moment in Europe's gay emancipation. A teacher becomes part of secret gay organisation Der Kreis, and tries to pursue his relationship with trans star Röbi Rapp against a backdrop of increasing police repression.

Music

Stoa
● Nik Bärtsch's Ronin, 2005

"Zen-funk"—as the Zurich pianist has baptised his genre—might just be the only suitable term. As much Steve Reich as it is James Brown, this album, by one of the city's finest jazz outfits, is one groovy exercise in restraint.

Claro Que Sí
● Yello, 1981

Founding member Carlos Perón's final album with the band planted a vital seed for the future of Euro-disco. Heavy on synths and cinematic tinges, this collection of landscapes goes from a rumble in the jungle to a rolling Western march—without ever straying too far from pop.

Liliput
● LiLiPut, 1982

Paving the way for countless aspiring girl groups around the world, the pop-punk band formerly known as Kleenex was listed in Kurt Cobain's top 50 favourite albums. One listen to songs like "Birdy" and "Tong Tong" from their first LP might help understand why.

© Culture
Ⓕ Food
Ⓝ Night
Ⓞ Outdoors
Ⓢ Shop

Kreis 1

Bodega Española
Münstergasse 15
+41 44 251 23 10
bodega-espanola.ch
→ p.15 Ⓕ

Cabaret Voltaire
Spiegelgasse 1
+41 43 268 57 20
cabaretvoltaire.ch
→ p.35 ©

Confiserie Sprüngli
Bahnhofstraße 21
+41 44 224 47 40
spruengli.ch
→ p.26 Ⓕ

EnSoie
Strehlgasse 26
+41 44 211 59 02
ensoie.com
→ p.33 Ⓢ

Flohmarkt Bürkliplatz
Bürkliplatz
+41 79 436 29 74
buerkli-flohmarkt.ch
→ p.16 Ⓢ

Frauenbadi
Stadthausquai
+41 44 211 95 92
→ p.11 Ⓞ

Giacometti Murals
Bahnhofquai 3
→ p.14 ©

Helmhaus
Limmatquai 31
+41 44 251 61 77
stadt-zuerich.ch
→ p.26 ©

Kaufleuten
Pelikanstrasse 18
+41 44 225 33 00
kaufleuten.ch
→ p.50 Ⓕ

Kronenhalle
Rämistraße 4
+41 44 262 99 00
kronenhalle.com
→ p.14, 26, 35, 50 Ⓕ

Kunsthaus Zürich
Heimplatz 1
+41 44 251 56 9
kunsthaus.ch
→ p.26, 33, 49 ©

Le Dézaley
Römergasse 7
+41 44 251 61 29
le-dezaley.ch
→ p.58 Ⓕ

Lima
Talacker 34
+41 44 225 33 75
limalima.ch
→ p.33 Ⓝ

Limited Stock
Spiegelgasse 22
+41 43 268 56 20
limited-stock.com
→ p.25 Ⓢ

Lumière
Widdergasse 5
+41 44 211 56 65
restaurant-lumiere.ch
→ p.8, 33

Milchbar
Kappelergasse 16
+41 44 211 90 12
milchbar.ch
→ p.58 Ⓕ

Neumarkt 17 AG
Neumarkt 17
+41 44 254 38 38
neumarkt17.ch
→ p.25 Ⓢ

Old Crow
Schwanengasse 4
+41 43 233 53 35
oldcrow.ch
→ p.50, 58 Ⓝ

Pavillon
Talstraße 1
+41 44 220 50 22
aupavillon.ch
→ p.33 Ⓕ

Pelikamo
Pelikanstraße 11
+41 44 210 04 06
pelikamo.com
→ p.33 Ⓢ

Rechberg
Chorgasse 20
+41 44 251 17 60
→ p.35 Ⓕ

Restaurant Bärengasse
Bahnhofstraße 25
+41 44 210 08 08
restaurant-
baerengasse.ch
→ p.33 Ⓕ

Rive Gauche
Talstraße 1
+41 44 220 50 60
agauche.ch
→ p.33 Ⓕ

Rooftop
Bahnhofstraße 74
+41 44 400 05 55
ooo-zh.ch
→ p.58 Ⓝ

Tales Bar
Selnaustrassse 29
+41 44 542 38 02
tales-bar.ch
→ p.58 Ⓝ

Taos
Augustinergasse 3
+41 44 448 11 22
taos-zurich.ch
→ p.33 Ⓕ

Tasoni
Sankt Peterstraße 1
+41 44 221 94 56
tasoni.com
→ p.16 Ⓢ

Terrasse
Limmatquai 3
+41 44 251 10 74
bindella.ch
→ p.33 Ⓕ

**Theaterhaus
Gessnerallee**
Gessnerallee 8
+41 44 225 81 10
gessnerallee.ch
→ p.35 ©

Tina Bar
Niederdorfstraße 10
+41 44 250 76 80
brasserie-louis.ch
→ p.35 Ⓝ

Townhouse
Weite Gasse 4
+41 43 843 70 00
ilovetownhouse.com
→ p.33 Ⓢ

Uhren Atelier
Rindermarkt 21
+41 44 262 60 90
uhrenatelier.ch
→ p.10 Ⓢ

Vestibule
Sankt Peterstraße 20
+41 44 260 13 31
vestibule.ch
→ p.33 Ⓢ

VMC
Rindermarkt 8
+41 44 251 56 96
vmcoriginal.com
→ p.10 Ⓢ

Widder Bar
Widdergasse 6
+41 44 224 24 11
widderhotel.com
→ p.33, 58 Ⓝ

Zeughauskeller
Bahnhofstraße 28A
+41 44 220 15 15
zeughauskeller.ch
→ p.57 Ⓕ

Zum Kropf
In Gassen 16
+41 44 221 18 05
zumkropf.ch
→ p.57 Ⓕ

Kreis 2

La Stanza
Bleicherweg 10
+41 43 817 62 82
lastanza.ch
→ p.26, 33 Ⓝ

Rote Fabrik
Seestraße 395
+41 44 485 58 58
rotefabrik.ch
→ p.50 ©

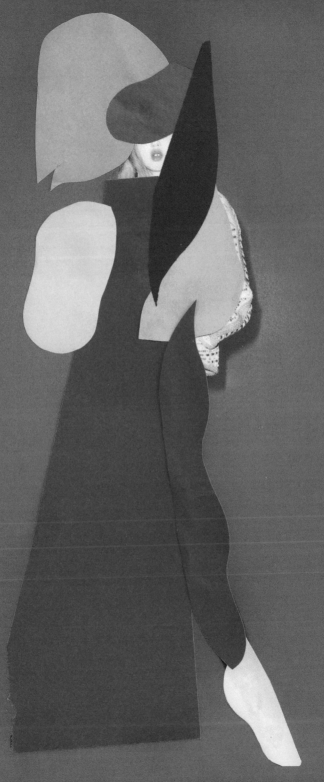

BIGZH.CH

Scheublein + Bak
Schloss Sihlberg,
Sihlberg 10
+41 43 888 55 10
scheubleinbak.com
→ p.33 ⓒ

Seebad Enge
Mythenquai 9
+41 44 201 38 89
seebadenge.ch
→ p.51 Ⓞ

Kreis 3

Bei Babette
Bertastraße 16
+41 43 366 85 02
beibabette.ch
→ p.20 Ⓕ

Beiz
Zweierstraße 114
+41 43 333 18 56
restaurant-beiz.ch
→ p.18 Ⓕ

Da Michelangelo
Gertrudstraße 37
+41 44 451 32 31
da-michelangelo.ch
→ p.15 Ⓕ

Daizy
Räffelstraße 28
+41 43 333 03 28
daizy.ch
→ p.19 Ⓕ

Ecco Zürich
Döltschiweg 234
+41 44 456 55 33
ecco-restaurant.ch
→ p.57 Ⓕ

Eco Design Home
Binzstraße 7
+41 44 450 33 80
ecodesignhome.ch
→ p.21 Ⓢ

Fein&Dein
Sihlfeldstraße 57
+41 79 328 46 32
feinunddeindesign.ch
→ p.20 Ⓢ

Friedhof Sihlfeld
Aemtlerstraße 151
+41 44 412 06 40
stadt-zuerich.ch
→ p.20 Ⓞ

**Herrmann Germann
Contemporary**
Stationsstraße 1
+41 44 450 27 80
herrmanngermann.com
→ p.26 ⓒ

Kulturfolger
Idastraße 46
kulturfolger.ch
→ p.20 ⓒ

Meyer's
Badenerstraße 219
+41 44 462 51 51
meyers-bar.ch
→ p.35 Ⓝ

Piazza
Idaplatz 2
+41 44 558 95 29
ida-piazza.ch
→ p.19 Ⓕ

Raygrodski
Sihlfeldstraße 49
+41 44 241 49 49
raygrodski.ch
→ p.20 Ⓝ

**Restaurant Bahnhof
Wiedikon**
Seebahnstraße 33
+41 44 462 64 24
beffa-gastro.ch
→ p.57 Ⓕ

Rost und Gold
Uetlibergstraße 15
+41 79 337 34 80
rostundgold.ch
→ p.21 Ⓢ

Vereinigung
Manessestraße 132
+41 44 462 01 48
vereinigung-barsol.ch
→ p.18 Ⓕ

Kreis 4

16 Tons
Anwandstraße 25
+41 44 242 02 03
16tons.ch
→ p.50 Ⓢ

Bank
Molkenstraße 15
+41 44 211 80 04
bankzuerich.ch
→ p.33, 53 Ⓕ

Bar 63
Rolandstraße 19
+41 44 241 75 83
bar63.ch
→ p.35, 50 Ⓝ

Berenik
Militärstraße 115
+41 77 427 78 36
berenik.ch
→ p.55 Ⓢ

Caduff's Wine Loft
Kanzleistraße 126
+41 44 240 22 55
wineloft.ch
→ p.55 Ⓕ

Club Zukunft
Dienerstraße 33
zukunft.cl
→ p.8, 35, 50 Ⓝ

El Lokal
Gessnerallee 11
+41 43 344 87 50
ellokal.ch
→ p.50 Ⓕ

EquiTable
Stauffacherstraße 163
+41 43 534 82 77
equi-table.ch
→ p.57 Ⓕ

**Fribourger
Fonduestübli**
Rotwandstraße 38
+41 44 241 90 76
fribourger-fondue-
stuebli.ch
→ p.35 Ⓕ

Gamper Restaurant
Nietengasse 1
+41 44 221 11 77
gamper-restaurant.ch
→ p.50, 58 Ⓕ

Gonzo
Langstraße 135
+41 43 317 99 25
gonzoclub.ch
→ p.55 Ⓝ

Grand Café Lochergut
Badenerstraße 230
+41 44 212 13 14
lochergut.net
→ p.19, 33, 50 Ⓕ

Happy Bäckerei
Dienerstraße 32
+41 43 243 97 80
happybeck.ch
→ p.52 Ⓢ

Longstreet
Langstraße 92
+41 44 241 21 72
longstreetbar.ch
→ p.16, 52 Ⓝ

**Männerbad
Schanzengraben**
Badweg 10
+41 44 211 95 94
→ p.11 Ⓞ

Metzg
Langstraße 31
+41 44 291 00 88
metzg-grill.ch
→ p.57 Ⓕ

Morgenstern
Zwinglistraße 27
+41 44 242 68 30
morgenstern-zh.ch
→ p.35, 49 Ⓕ

**Museum Haus
Konstruktiv**
Selnaustraße 25
+41 44 217 70 80
hauskonstruktiv.ch
→ p.26 ⓒ

Olé-Olé-Bar
Langstraße 138
+41 44 242 91 39
oleolebar.ch
→ p.35, 52 Ⓝ

OOR Records
Anwandstraße 30
+41 44 542 32 80
oor-rec.ch
→ p.50 Ⓢ

Palestine Grill
Langstraße 92
palestinegrill.tumblr.
com
→ p.35, 52 Ⓕ

Pergola
Kanzleistraße 121
+41 44 241 12 21
pergola-ristorante.ch
→ p.57 Ⓕ

Ristorante Italia
Zeughausstraße 61
+41 43 233 88 44
ristorante-italia.ch
→ p.35 Ⓕ

Soeder
Ankerstrasse 124
+41 44 558 34 43
soeder.ch
→ p.54 Ⓢ

Sport Bar
Kanzleistraße 76
+41 43 317 91 09
sport-bar.ch
→ p.49 Ⓕ

Total Bar
Tellstraße 19
+41 44 242 49 69
→ p.35 Ⓝ

Volkshaus
Stauffacherstraße 60
+41 44 242 11 55
restaurantvolkshaus.ch
→ p.15, 50 Ⓕ

**Carhartt WIP
Stores Zürich**

**Spitalgasse 2
8001 Zürich
Lagerstraße 1
8004 Zürich**

WORK IN PROGRESS

www.carhartt-wip.com

Welschland
Zweierstraße 56
+41 43 243 98 50
welschland.com
→ p.58, 60 (F)

Zero Zero Rare Groove
Bäckerstraße 54
+41 44 241 85 20
zerozero.ch
→ p.50

Zum Goldenen Fass
Zwinglistraße 7
+41 44 242 47 66
zumgoldenenfass.ch
→ p.35 (F)

Kreis 5

25hours Hotel
Pfingstweidstraße 102
+41 44 577 25 25
25hours-hotels.com
→ p.24 (C)

Buchhandlung Kunstgriff
Limmatstraße 270
+41 44 272 90 66
kunstgriff.ch
→ p.16 (S)

Café Noir
Neugasse 33
+41 44 558 34 10
cafe-noir.ch
→ p.49, 54 (F)

Freitag Flagship Store
Geroldstraße 17
+41 43 366 95 20
freitag.ch
→ p.25 (S)

Helsinkiklub
Geroldstraße 35
helsinkiklub.ch
→ p.35 (N)

Im Viadukt
Viaduktstraße
im-viadukt.ch
→ p.25, 54 (S)

Josef
Gasometerstraße 24
+41 44 271 65 95
josef.ch
→ p.26 (F)

Les Halles
Pfingstweidstraße 6
+41 44 273 11 25
les-halles.ch
→ p.54 (F)

Little Black Dress
Josefstr. 45
+41 43 540 16 70
littleblackdress.ch
→ p.33 (S)

Löwenbräukunst
Limmatstraße 270
westbau.com
→ p.26, 49

Markthalle
Limmatstraße 231
+41 44 201 00 60
im-viadukt.ch
→ p.15, 54 (F)

Moods
Schiffbauplatz
+41 44 276 80 00
moods.club
→ p.50 (N)

Museum für Gestaltung
Pfingstweidstraße 96
+41 43 446 67 67
museum-gestaltung.ch
→ p.9, 24 (C)

Museum of Digital Art
Pfingstweidstraße 101
+41 44 456 40 50
muda.co → p.11 (C)

Panama
Lettensteg 10
+41 76 397 79 71
panamabar.ch
→ p.49 (N)

Restaurant Eisenhof
Gasometerstraße 20
+41 44 271 39 90
restauranteisenhof.ch
→ p.53 (F)

Rosso
Geroldstraße 31
+41 43 818 22 54
restaurant-rosso.ch
→ p.55 (F)

Sala of Tokyo
Limmatstraße 29
+41 44 271 52 90
sala-of-tokyo.ch
→ p.15 (F)

Teo Jakob
Limmatstraße 266
+41 44 222 09 30
teojakob.ch
→ p.25 (S)

Waldraud
Josefstraße 142
+41 44 554 60 50
waldraud.com
→ p.55 (S)

Kreis 6

Thomas Ammann
Restelbergstraße 97
+41 44 360 51 60
ammannfineart.com
→ p.14 (C)

Kreis 7

Justus
Asylstraße 70
+41 44 380 21 81
justus-roemerhof.ch
→ p.33 (S)

Luca²
Asylstraße 81
+41 44 252 03 53
→ p.16 (F)

Spa at The Dolder Grand
Kurhausstraße 65
+41 44 456 60 00
thedoldergrand.com
→ p.51 (O)

The Restaurant at The Dolder Grand
Kurhausstraße 65
+41 44 456 60 00
thedoldergrand.com
→ p.59 (F)

Wirtschaft Degenried
Degenriedstraße 135
+41 44 381 51 80
degenried.ch
→ p.8, 26, 50 (F)

Zoo Zürich
Zürichbergstraße 221
+41 44 254 25 00
zoo.ch
→ p.7 (O)

Kreis 8

Bimi
Seefeldstraße 25
+41 43 243 77 77
swissbimi.ch
→ p.15 (F)

Kornsilo
Seefeldstraße 231
+41 44 389 90 67
kornsilo.ch
→ p.33 (F)

Modestrom
Seefeldstraße 110
+41 43 499 98 80
modestrom.com
→ p.33 (S)

Obere Flühgasse
Flühgasse 69
+41 44 381 11 10
→ p.15 (F)

Seebad Utoquai
Utoquai
+41 44 251 61 51
→ p.11 (O)

Kreis 9

Up State
Flüelastraße 54
up-state.ch
→ p.14 (C)

Kreis 10

Karma International
Hönggerstraße 40
+41 43 535 85 91
karmainternational.org
→ p.14, 33 (C)

Restaurant Die Waid
Waidbadstraße 45
+41 43 422 08 08
diewaid.ch
→ p.50 (F)

Unterer Letten
Wasserwerkstraße 141
+41 44 362 10 80
stadt-zuerich.ch
→ p.25 (O)

Outskirts

Galerie Bruno Bischofberger
Weissenrainstraße 1, Männedorf
+41 44 250 77 77
brunobischofberger.com → p.14 (C)

Gasthof zur Sonne
Seestraße 37, Stäfa
+41 43 477 10 10
sonnestaefa.ch
→ p.10, 58 (F)

Restaurant Neuhof
Sternenstraße 30, Bachs
+41 44 858 11 80
neuhof-bachs.ch
→ p.26 (F)

Seebad Katzensee
Katzenseestraße, Kreis 11
+41 44 371 08 90
→ p.11 (O)

You
Dufaux-straße 1, Opfikon
+41 44 525 50 00
kamehagrandzuerich.com → p.58 (F)

Also available from LOST iN

Next Issue: Miami

LOSTIN.COM

THOMAS MEYER   DEM VERGESSEN
ZUMINDEST ZIEMLICH NAHE

Story

Close to Oblivion

Thomas Meyer

Over Zurich, the light is vanishing. You could say it's a beautiful sight how the Alps beyond the lake dusk into a deep blue, while the clouds in the west travel in an orange glow. But then again, a lot of things are nice to look at, especially at nightfall. Anna for instance. Twenty-nine, curly hazelnut hair, big pond-green eyes and a body whose charms are only multiplied by her sharp wardrobe. It is obvious what men think on seeing her. But even women think: "If I ever… Then it would be with Anna."

All these thoughts ascend into the evening sky above the outdoor bar as Anna enters. Conversations mute. Men's elbows discreetly bump into men's ribs, women's eyes spray a small dose of poison. Anna moves towards a young man, nervously sipping a beer at one of the bar tables. Upon seeing her, his anxiety only rises higher. His name is Philipp and he's been head over heels with Anna for two weeks now. When other men realise Anna is here to meet Philipp, their stares turn equally hostile.

Philipp is asking himself if this is the day she'll finally sleep with him. He just can't tell. This is their third date (so maybe yes) but all of his raunchier text messages fell into an unresponsive void (so maybe no). Of course Anna knows if she will sleep with Philipp tonight. If he only stopped wearing that yearning stare and ceased those clumsy attempts to impress her. But then again no guy ever managed that. No guy ever saw past her looks and into her soul. As if she existed only as a woman, not as a person. Philipp greets Anna anxiously and in an instant she's bored. At least a part of her. The other part has exactly what it came for.

Men have reacted to her like this for a long time now. And everybody—man and woman alike—thinks the reception she gets is a blessing. A gift. But not Anna. She hates it. She hates that men want to own her, to consume her. She's hated it since 1995, when her grandpa started his nighttime visits.

Anna doesn't remember much about that time. Those years before 1999 when the old man—to Anna's secret delight—suddenly dropped dead, are almost entirely wiped from memory. She only remembers the image of him standing in the frame of her door, with that strange predatory look on his face. And that her mother later said that time would better rest in peace. Funny, because peace would be the last word to describe the pitch-black sea, if it were storm-ridden like this. But Anna trusted her mother and buried the shame, along with her own light in the dark. And she forgot. Or at least came close to forgetting. Close to oblivion.

But Anna can pinpoint the exact moment when she realised she had to retake control of her body. Men had been staring at her for a while and she'd always looked at the ground. But shortly after her 14th birthday, there was a man at school, who stared at her, which she liked. She smiled at him, talked to him and suddenly she knew. Knew she could have everything from him. Everything. Just like that. Why, she asked herself. He didn't even know her. But then she understood. He didn't want to know her. He wanted something else. It was only up to her to decide if he'd get it. Her decision alone.

And so Anna—who had been consumed all those times—began consuming herself. One man after the other. She played with them, consumed them and washed them down with alcohol.

Today she'll consume Philipp, who cannot take his eyes off her breasts, let alone stop saying things supposed to be charming and funny. Sigh.

Philipp brings more drinks from the bar. If it were up to him they'd have left long ago, to do those things he's been picturing for days now. But Anna—especially in the light of those things—could use more Prosecco. While Philipp talks about something, she tries to remember the last time this was different. She doesn't need to think hard. With Marco, of course.

Of course Marco stared at her breasts too, but mostly into her eyes. And of course Marco also talked about himself, but mostly asked about her. When she realised Marco was on a date with a person, not just a woman, with her, Anna, and she was on a date with him, Marco—she became scared. If he came this close to her now, how close could he get to her? To her oblivion?

She didn't take Marco home. What a sad compliment, not to sleep with somebody.

Darkness takes over the Zurich sky, with multicoloured lights everywhere. It is nice to look at. As are other things. Anna for instance, as she walks with Philipp along the river. She locks arms with him, hips slowly dandling, curls moving along, while Philipp flexes his muscles. Tonight he'll get what he wants and so will Anna. Philipp wants sex with Anna. Anna wants power and control. But really she wants something else. And while she walks with a man who cannot give it to her, she realises it may have been forever taken from her.

Zurich-born Thomas Meyer earned his first accolades as a writer for Zurich underground magazine "Kult", and published his first novel in 2012. His latest work is a collection of short stories containing 144 insights into a wide array of topics from dead plants to business-savvy non-Jews

Zurich
Zurich
Zurich

THE BEST
TIPS ARE
BENEATH
THE SURFACE

...discover them in the LOST iN mobile app

LOST iN